Guide to Handraising Puppies

Janice A. Koler-Matznick

Contents

PHOTO CREDITS

Photographs and Illustrations: Isabelle Francais, Janice A. Koler, and Robert Pearcy

© T.F.H. Publications, Inc.

Distributed in the UNITED STATES to the Pet Trade by T.F.H. Publications, Inc., One T.F.H. Plaza, Neptune City, NJ 07753; on the Internet at www.tfh.com; in CANADA Rolf C. Hagen Inc., 3225 Sartelon St. Laurent-Montreal Quebec H4R 1E8; Pet Trade by H & L Pet Supplies Inc., 27 Kingston Crescent, Kitchener, Ontario N2B 2T6; in ENGLAND by T.F.H. Publications, PO Box 74, Havant PO9 5TT; in AUSTRALIA AND THE SOUTH PACIFIC by T.F.H. (Australia), Pty. Ltd., Box 149, Brookvale 2100 N.S.W., Australia; in NEW ZEALAND by Brooklands Aquarium Ltd. 5 McGiven Drive, New Plymouth, RD1 New Zealand; in SOUTH AFRICA, Rolf C. Hagen S.A. (PTY.) LTD. P.O. Box 201199, Durban North 4016, South Africa; in Japan by T.F.H. Publications, Japan—Jiro Tsuda, 10-12-3 Ohjidai, Sakura, Chiba 285, Japan. Published by T.F.H. Publications, Inc.
MANUFACTURED IN THE
UNITED STATES OF AMERICA
BY T.F.H. PUBLICATIONS, INC.

INTRODUCTION

Raising orphan and one-puppy litters into healthy, well-adjusted dogs presents unique challenges. The medical, nutritional, and psychological aspects of puppy development that nature normally takes care of all must be managed under totally artificial conditions, sometimes by people with little experience with newborn puppies. This comprehensive instruction manual is devoted to handraising puppies and emphasizes the importance of providing for the healthy social and psychological development of orphan puppies, especially for single puppies being raised alone. The handrearing suggestions offered are useful to owners raising large litters that need to be supplemented and for those who have puppies needing extra care, such as weak puppies or runts that have trouble competing with their stronger siblings.

A successful attempt to handfeed can bring great satisfaction, and failure is hard to accept. Human hearts seem to naturally go out to the "underdog," the runt valiantly struggling, the puppy with a problem. One of the hardest tasks of handfeeding is accepting that despite heroic efforts, there may

Early in life most puppies receive all of their nourishment from their mothers.

Dogs are a very important part of their owner's lives and the bond between humans and animals is a strong one.

should take the dog to a licensed veterinarian for a complete checkup, including a fecal exam. In the case of young puppies, an ounce of prevention is indeed worth much more than a pound of cure. An undiagnosed medical problem or physical defect can mean wasted time, money, and unnecessary animal suffering, not to mention human grief and guilt over a death or illness that might have been prevented.

This newborn Bichon Frise puppy will need special care if his mother is unable or unwilling to nurse him.

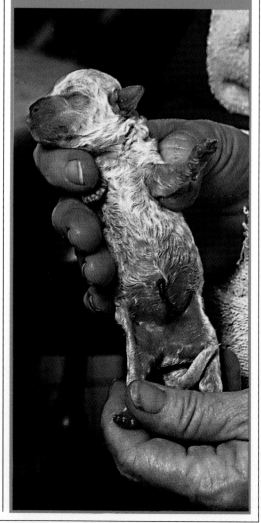

be failure, especially with puppies that started out weak or ill. At some point, when the puppy is obviously not thriving, the caregiver should consult with their veterinarian and decide if it is time to euthanize the puppy. This might be more humane than allowing him to keep fighting a downhill battle he has little chance of winning, especially if he is likely to have permanent handicaps or health problems that would prevent him from living a normal, active life.

This book should be used in conjunction with veterinary consultation. Anyone who is planning to breed their female dog, who finds themselves with an already pregnant dog, or rescues an abandoned puppy

FOSTERING PUPPIES

Before you take on the job of handraising a litter or a single puppy, try to find a canine foster mother. A healthy and willing foster dam will provide the proper natural environment for the critical first three to four weeks of the puppy's life. Try to find someone willing to cooperate who has a dam with puppies of approximately the same age and size. Ask friends, local dog clubs, and veterinarians if they know of any potential foster dams.

Interview the potential foster dam's owner and look at the area where the dam and her puppies are kept. The nursery should be warm, draft-free, dry, and quiet, away from the main traffic and activity areas of the house or kennel, but it need not be sterile. The puppies should be in a small space with safe bedding, like the whelping boxes and puppy pens that are described later in this book. If the dam is doing a good job and has a healthy milk supply, her puppies ought to rest quietly when she is not nursing or cleaning them and the puppy pen should be free of puppy droppings. The dam's coat may be showing the wear and tear of being a mother, but she should be of good weight, have bright eyes,

Excellent mothers, like this long-haired Chihuahua, are good candidates for fostering.

Your dam and her puppies will look to you, the owner, for support and care.

It will be adequate for a normal dam. Offer to provide the owner compensation for the extra food required for the dam to nurse more puppies, to assist with the care of the puppies, and to supply a fair share of the puppy-weaning food. Agree on an age for weaning and on a date for you to take the fostered puppy or puppies home.

Remember, dogs do not always behave in predictable ways and accidents can happen. Introducing strange puppies into a litter is taking a calculated risk. If, after a careful introduction and apparent acceptance by the foster dam, some or all of the puppies are injured or killed by the dam or other unforeseen accidents happen, the owner of the dam cannot be held liable. This should be discussed and, along with any other conditions, agreed upon,

and be current on vaccinations. To avoid unnecessary stress on the dam, do not handle her puppies and pet her only if she comes to you in an obviously friendly manner. Even the most outgoing female may become wary of strangers while she has young puppies, and this natural behavior change while she feels she is "on duty" must be respected.

If everything seems in order and the foster dam's owner appears to be a person with whom you can work, ask about the type of food the dam is being fed, and if she gets any supplements. Many dog owners have their own favorite brand of dog food, and as long as it is labeled "complete and balanced for all life stages," do not worry if it is not what you prefer feeding.

This black Lab dam is not only the proud parent of her own puppies, but it looks as if she's adopted a few Dalmatians as well!

This Pekingese dam has no trouble nursing her one-day-old puppies as well as her two-week-old mixed-breed foster puppy.

put in writing, and signed by both parties before the fostering experiment is attempted.

INTRODUCTION OF PUPPIES TO A FOSTER DAM

Unless the nursing dam is exceptionally calm and outgoing when strangers are around her puppies, her owner should be the only one to attempt the introduction of the orphan puppies. Before bringing the puppies into contact with the foster dam, rub a damp cloth over her teats and her puppies; then, just before introducing the puppies, wipe the orphans down with the cloth to transfer the familiar scents to them. Bring the orphan(s) next to the puppy box in a covered or enclosed container. Using slow, deliberate motions and talking in a soothing monotone, present the puppies one at a time with their rears toward the dam. The presenter should have most of the puppy covered by their hands at first. If the bitch shows no aggression or extreme excitement, slowly uncover the puppy while she examines him, praising her for her calm response and interest. Have her lie down and place the puppy between her front feet, keeping one hand in contact with the puppy while petting the head and stroking the muzzle of the bitch. This puts the presenter in a good defensive position if the bitch takes offense and tries to snap at the puppy. Slowly remove the hand from the puppy and allow the bitch to examine the pup while he crawls about. If the dam is calm, and the puppy is crawling in the correct direction, let him find a teat on his own. If necessary, place the pup on a teat. A few drops of milk may have to be squeezed into the puppy's mouth to get him to take a nipple. Give the pup some support and help him to stay on the nipple while he learns proper nursing motions. To help keep the dam calm during introductions, her own puppies should be kept with her. Removing them could raise her anxiety level.

Be very careful, especially with breeds that are often dog aggressive, and stay right next to the dam and puppies until it is

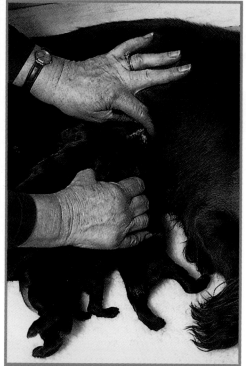

A newly introduced puppy may need some help in beginning the nursing process, but should catch on quickly.

Once the dam has carefully inspected the newcomer, licking and sniffing him for a time, she should accept him and relax.

certain the dam will not act aggressively toward the newcomers. Keep her under observation for at least an hour or until she has licked the newcomers and relaxed while they nurse before leaving her unattended.

If the added puppies mean the bitch will be nursing more than six puppies, after the first two weeks you may want to supplement with one or two handfeedings per day until weaning, which can begin at three weeks of age. The nursing dam should be offered increasing amounts of high-quality dog food as the puppies grow, enough so that she is not losing her body fat to produce milk.

THE PROPER HANDRAISING ENVIRONMENT

Puppies arrive in a very immature state. Nature has designed them to live the first three weeks entirely in a dark enclosed space—the den. They are born with just those attributes required to survive in this sheltered environment under the care of their dam. Most of their voluntary nervous system and portions of their involuntary nervous system, such as sight, hearing, elimination, and internal temperature regulation, are not operating at birth. If pregnancy was extended until these puppy systems could be fully operational, the dam would have difficulty hunting in the wild, due to her increased size, and she could be in a weakened state at whelping. Most of a fetal puppy's accumulation of muscle and fat occur during the last three weeks before birth, so the dam's agility and therefore her hunting ability, is not impaired for the first two thirds of her pregnancy. Because newborn puppies are so immature, they have well-defined environmental needs.

TEMPERATURE REGULATION

The most imperative need of a newborn is external temperature regulation. A puppy can raise his

Puppies come into the world nearly helpless and need a special environment in order to develop into healthy adults.

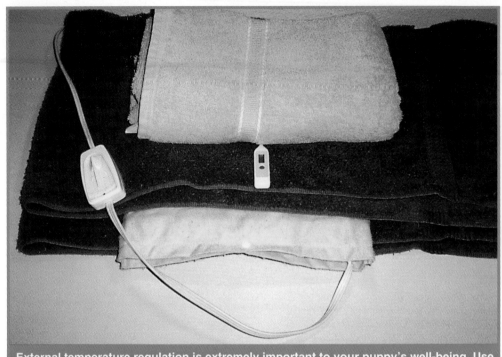

External temperature regulation is extremely important to your puppy's well-being. Use a thermometer to test the temperature of the heating pad your puppy will be using.

body temperature a maximum of 12 degrees above the air temperature around him. When the body temperature drops below 94 degrees Fahrenheit, hypothermia begins and puppies cannot nurse properly. Sometimes when a person finds that a puppy has become chilled, they try to warm him by giving him warm milk in an eyedropper. At 94 degrees Fahrenheit, however, the digestive system shuts down, and the milk will just ferment in the stomach and add to the puppy's physiological stress.

In nature, this warm environment is supplied by the den enclosure and the bodies of the dam and littermates. With an orphan or single puppy litter, you must be ready to provide a safe and reliable source of warmth.

Most experts believe the external temperature around a puppy should be about 90 degrees Fahrenheit for the first week and should be reduced about five degrees Fahrenheit a week until 75 degrees is reached, then held at this temperature until at least six weeks of age. These temperatures allow normal growth and digestion to take place. At about two weeks, the puppy's own internal thermostat starts to operate, but until then his only temperature regulating response is to crawl toward warmth and to vocalize—cry for attention—when chilled.

There are several methods of providing this external warmth. Before trying any of them, get a good thermometer and use it to test the actual heat of the surface

A heating pad covered by a soft blanket is a perfect resting spot for your puppy.

on which the puppy will be lying. If the heat source is underneath the pup, remember to put a cover, such as a folded towel, heavy

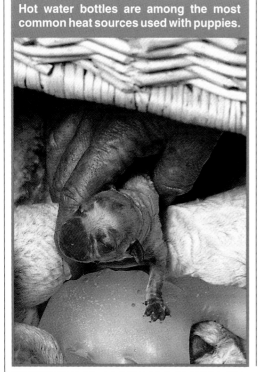

Hot water bottles are among the most common heat sources used with puppies.

cloth, or small pillow, over the thermometer when you do this test, because the temperature can quickly build up between a body and an underlying heat source and cause severe burns.

Some of the most common heat sources used are electric heating pads, hot water bottles, and heat lamps. Any human-type heating pad should be wrapped in a double layer of toweling to provide some air circulation between the puppy and the pad. A heating pad used specifically for puppies should be labeled "waterproof." Most of the human pads I have used needed to be on the lowest setting, with two towels laid over it, in order to approximate 90 degrees on a covered thermometer. Heat pads, usually of molded materials, that are designed for dogs or pigs should be equipped with a rheostat control so that the heat level can

Infrared panels should be wall-mounted or hung above a whelping box to assist with temperature regulation.

be adjusted. Molded pads should be covered only with very porous materials, because they will warp if the heat builds up on the surface.

Heat lamps produce hot spots and should never be aimed directly at the puppy but offset enough to prevent overheating. It is best to use a red bulb because this is non-irritating to the puppy's eyes when they first begin to open.

Infrared heat sources, which are used with all types of animals but are often found in the reptile or bird section of pet stores, give off no visible light and provide a "sun-like" heat. The long infrared warming rays penetrate into muscle tissue and warm the body and softer materials like wood and plaster, not the surrounding air space. Ceramic infrared heating elements, shaped like a regular heat or spot bulb, become hot to the touch and should only be used with a heat or spot lamp

holder that is rated for high heat. Infrared panels, which resemble acoustic ceiling tiles, are about one inch thick, come in various sizes, and are safe to touch, as they do not get hot. They can be mounted over or next to the puppy box in several ways.

Newborn pups can crawl about to adjust their temperature. Any source of external heat should be arranged so that there is a temperature gradient, with a warmer section, either directly on the pad or under the edge of the light's central area, and a cooler section, such as an area not covered by the pad or light. This will allow the pup to move to the cooler spot if he gets too hot. If the room air temperature is much below 75 degrees Fahrenheit, a loose cloth cover should be

Puppies will stay together to keep warm. If you have a single-puppy litter, you must be sure your pup's temperature is regulated.

provided over at least part of the puppy box to create a still air space around the pup. A cover is a must whenever there is a draft, as puppies lose body heat when exposed to a draft. This can be life threatening to a newborn.

In an emergency, your own body heat can be used to warm the puppy. Put on a knit top, like a sweatshirt or heavy T-shirt, tuck it in to a snug waistband or put a belt or tie a cord over the bottom portion of the shirt, and put the pup in the pouch that will form above the belt next to your skin. Leave the pup there as long as necessary. He will be kept at the perfect temperature and will sleep through your movements.

Milk jugs or glass containers can be filled with hot water, wrapped in cloth to prevent scalding tender puppy skin, and placed around the pup. If nothing else is available, the heat given off by a working television, stereo speaker, etc. can be utilized by placing the puppy in a small box on top of such a device.

Remember to *test the temperature* and be sure the air vents on the electronic equipment are not blocked or everything will overheat, including the pup.

HUMIDITY

Ideally, humidity in the puppy box should be about 55–65 percent to prevent drying of the skin and dehydration, especially if you are using artificial heat sources like electric pads or lamps. You can raise the local humidity simply by placing a wide container of water, such as a pie plate, next to the puppy box. If the air is exceedingly dry, such as in a desert climate, you may have to place a dampened cloth over part of the puppy box or use a humidifier or vaporizer to increase the evaporation. Do not place any

This little guy cuddles comfortably on a heat pad with his stuffed buddy.

uncovered containers of water inside the box because even a newborn moves around enough for it to spill.

Inexpensive instruments for measuring relative humidity are available in hardware, houseware, and garden departments of most discount stores. Look in the

bedding is not loose enough for the pup to get covered, as the bitch might accidentally jump or step on him, causing injury. This is usually not a problem with small breeds, however. The bitch will probably want to dig around in her "whelping den," but she will not be stressed if loose bedding is

When choosing a whelping box for your dam consider her size, the expected size of her litter, as well as the size of her puppies.

reptile section of the pet store for humidity detectors and temperature detectors designed for use with reptiles.

If the puppy's thin delicate skin does get dry and flaky, massage in a few drops of baby oil. Do not go overboard and saturate the coat, as this promotes chilling.

BEDDING

If the dam or foster mother is attending the pup, be sure the

not provided. She will go through the motions anyway, releasing the emotional tension that is created by the need to express an instinct.

If the pup is not being dam-raised, you can use old towels or any soft cloth for bedding the first two weeks. After two weeks, bedding material texture becomes important because the pup starts to crawl about more. Indoor-outdoor carpeting with an open-weave backing is ideal. With

Puppies are often kept on newspaper because it is absorbent and easy to clean up.

papers placed underneath, any urine will pass through and away from the pup and be absorbed for easy cleaning. Be sure the carpet is stiff enough not to bunch up, and cut it to fit the area neatly. Avoid ragged edges or holes that might catch on baby nails and unravel and tangle the pup. Make two carpets to alternate for cleaning.

Wash all carpets before use, rinse with a solution of one tablespoon of household bleach to one gallon of water, or follow directions on any disinfectant that will kill viruses. Then let sit for 15 minutes and rinse *thoroughly* with clear water. When you think you have rinsed it well, continue for another couple minutes just to be sure. You can lay carpet out on cement or grass areas (bleach might kill some grasses) and use the hose. If you are using bedding that can be washed in the machine, add the disinfectant to the wash cycle, estimating how many gallons of water the machine holds in order to dilute to the proper solution, and use a second rinse cycle. Puppies, with their sensitive skins, and even older dogs can develop rashes and other health problems if they are in prolonged contact with detergent or chemical residues, organic wastes such as urine, or damp surfaces, so be as certain as possible the bedding is always clean and dry.

Newspaper should only be used with puppies older than three weeks of age because it provides poor footing for nursing puppies still building strength. Also, the ink on newspapers easily rubs off and makes light-colored pups dirty. If you must use newspaper, then place several layers flat on the bottom of the puppy area and cover with a couple of inches of paper torn into long strips. This provides some traction, and, if the dam is no longer cleaning up after the pup or if he is an orphan pup, the stools and wet spots then tend to get "buried" away from direct contact.

Newsprint and other dirt

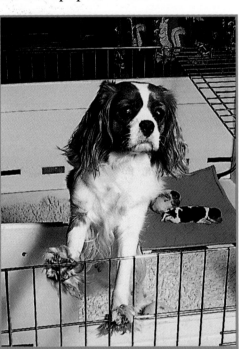

Your dam will be spending at least four weeks in her whelping box—make sure she's comfortable!

can be "dry" cleaned off a puppy's coat by rubbing with a damp cloth and then applying cornstarch to the damp fur. The cornstarch is then brushed or rubbed out, leaving a much cleaner coat. There are also commercial dry and liquid waterless shampoos made for cats that do an excellent job. If you can only find waterless shampoo for dogs, be sure the

label says it is all right to use on young puppies, or contact the manufacturer and ask them directly.

WHELPING AND PUPPY BOXES

One piece of equipment that every dog breeder should have is a whelping or puppy box. The box should be constructed so that it can serve as the den for at least four weeks. Boxes that are meant for use by the dam must be no smaller than one length of the dam measured from the top of the head to the base of the tail. The sides need to be high enough to confine the puppies when they start to walk around.

A frame around the outside of the box made of pipes, wood, or any convenient material, or even a card table placed over the box and covered with a blanket or cloth on three sides, would create a more natural den. Feeling enclosed psychologically comforts some new mothers, especially those with their first litter. If your bitch is reluctant to stay in the box or seems jumpy and nervous, try providing some type of visual

This large appliance box has been fashioned into a puppy/whelping box with top flaps that open for easy access.

barrier, such as a screen made of wood or a sheet draped over a line between the puppy box and the rest of the room.

If you are going to paint the box, use high-gloss latex enamel. This surface is easily scrubbed and will hold up well under frequent cleaning.

It is not necessary, nor even desirable, that the nest or whelping box be kept "germ free." Chemical residues from disinfectants and detergents are sources of potential health problems, so use these sparingly and carefully after the initial cleaning. The most important consideration is maintaining basically clean, dry bedding.

A bumper rail around the inside of the box is used to prevent large-breed dams from accidentally crushing a new pup into the side. This "pig rail" must be low enough to connect with the dam's back when she is lying down, but high enough—at least four inches—for the pup to fit under. It may be removed after the first week or so, depending on how strong the pup is. An easily removable bumper can be made of three-inch diameter PVC pipe and 4 three-way corner connections.

If the side is constructed as tall as the elbows of the dam, she will be able to step in. Before the puppies can walk, one side may be lower for her easy entry. This will help reduce the risk of accidental injury to the pups from the dam jumping into the box. For this reason, one side of a

This is a good example of how to construct a well-made whelping box.

Whelping / Puppy Box Plan

Collapsible Homemade Type
1/2" Plywood

Top View

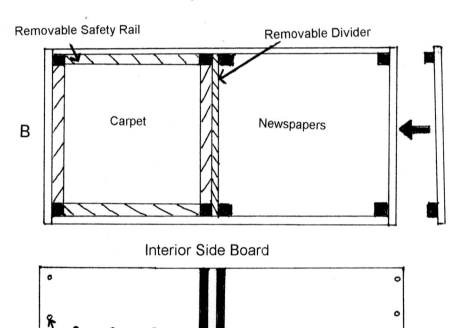

Removable Safety Rail

Removable Divider

Carpet

Newspapers

B

Interior Side Board

Drilled For Screw Assembly

Floor rests on 2 X 2" frame

2 Boards This End - Remove top one to allow dam easy access until pups can climb.

End Board B
(Whelping Side)

If you do not provide your dam with an actual puppy box, you must secure a designated area of your home for the new family.

whelping box usually has two pieces, either hinged together or left separate, and placed into a slot for easy removal.

If the puppies are of a very large breed, they will soon need more room to walk around, so the box can be made extra long and a divider inserted to create a smaller neonatal/whelping area. When the puppies are walking, the den half can be left with regular bedding, and the other half can be filled with newspaper or pine shavings. The divider can be removed or replaced with a low board that the puppies can step over. This is a good idea even for small breeds, as with this arrangement the early habit of leaving the den to eliminate, which all normal puppies attempt to do by instinct starting around two weeks of age, is reinforced and a solid foundation is set for

later housetraining. If the sides are high enough that the bitch's teats drag across when she enters the box, a pad made from the foam sections used to insulate pipes will usually fit right over the edge and will prevent possible injury.

If there is no way to have a special box made for orphan puppies, there are a multitude of alternatives that can be used, limited only by your imagination. For small-breed puppies, a dresser drawer, basket, or cardboard box is adequate when there are only one or two puppies, providing there is enough room for them to get away from the hottest spot if they need to. For larger breeds, cut-down major appliance boxes, moving boxes, or the large, square, wooden bins used in orchards to hold fruit can be put to use.

HAND FEEDING

If it is at all possible, the newborn puppy should nurse from his mother or another dam that has puppies only a day or two old for at least two days. During this three-day period, the first milk produced, called colostrum, supplies the puppy with antibodies from the dam's immune system. These antibodies will protect the newborn from common contagious diseases for a few weeks. If nursing is not possible, then ask your veterinarian about giving the puppy vaccinations at an early age.

If handrearing is necessary because the dam refuses to let the puppy nurse, tie a gauze strip or nylon stocking around her muzzle or use a purchased muzzle. Force her to lie down and allow the puppy to nurse about four times a day for 15 minutes at a time for at least three days. Keep track of the puppy's weight gain as explained later, and supplement as needed.

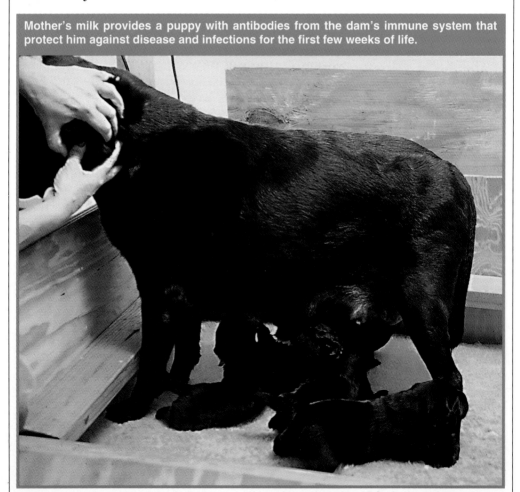

Mother's milk provides a puppy with antibodies from the dam's immune system that protect him against disease and infections for the first few weeks of life.

Muzzle

Tie on top of the nose, cross under the jaw, and tie tightly behind the ears.

If a dam becomes defensive or aggressive, it may be necessary to muzzle her so the puppies can attempt nursing.

If there is more than one puppy that must be handfed in the litter, the puppies should be checked several times daily for sore or swollen spots created when puppies suck on each other. If this occurs, separate the puppies by a partition in their box for about two weeks.

FORMULAS FOR HANDFEEDING

Cow milk by itself is not a suitable substitute for bitch's milk. It has only about half the proteins, calories, calcium, and phosphorous that bitch's milk contains and is much more dilute. It also has a higher lactose (milk sugar) content, and puppies normally do not have enough of the enzyme lactase to digest that much lactose, resulting in diarrhea.

There are several commercial bitch milk replacements available. They are sold by veterinarians, pet supply stores, and sometimes by feed stores or supermarkets. These formulas are readily accepted by puppies, will not cause diarrhea, and are available in powdered or liquid form. Follow label directions, and refrigerate any unused portions in a tightly closed container. If you are expecting puppies, you should purchase one of these milk replacements before the whelping date to have on hand, just in case.

In comparison to mother's milk, cow's milk cannot suitably nourish a growing puppy.

Table 1. Comparison of Milk Composition (%)

	Cow	Bitch
Lactose	4.80	3.10
Protein	3.30	8.00
Fat	3.80	9.00
Minerals	0.71	0.90
Total Solids	12.61	21.00

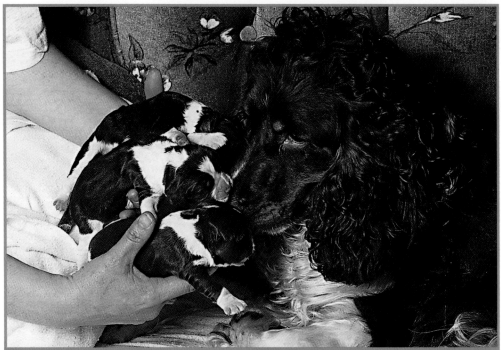

Finding a foster mother is the best possible solution if your dam refuses to nurse her puppies.

In an emergency, there are other substitutes that can be used until a commercial formula can be obtained. They should not be used exclusively, as they are deficient in the protein arginine. If this protein is too low in the diet of nursing puppies, they can develop cataracts. The first emergency substitute is goat's milk. Goat's milk, while not perfect for any animal other than a goat kid, is more easily digestible and has lower lactose content than cow's milk. It has been used successfully for puppies, kittens, rabbits, human babies, and several other species. Many supermarkets and nearly all health food stores carry goat's milk in refrigerated cartons or in condensed form in cans.

Breeders and veterinarians have successfully used the emergency formulas below.

EMERGENCY FEEDING FORMULAS

Mix, cover, and keep refrigerated for no more than *24 hours* before use.

Formula 1

1 can evaporated milk + 1/3 can water

yolk of one egg (no white — not digestible)

1 Tablespoon clear Karo syrup (optional)

Formula 2

1 cup whole milk

1 teaspoon salad oil

2 egg yolks

1 drop liquid puppy vitamins (optional)

Formula 3

   13 oz boiled water

   13 oz evaporated milk

   8 oz plain yogurt with active cultures

   1 egg yolk

   1 jar strained baby meat

   Blend well and strain though cheese cloth.

   Karo syrup acts as a mild laxative, so discontinue if

puppy's nursing drive. Some behaviorists believe that if a puppy is fed only by a tube he will tend to become a chewer as he matures in an attempt to attain the oral gratification he lacked as an infant. Whether that is true or not, the more natural nursing action of bottle feeding certainly does provide the puppy with physically beneficial exercise and

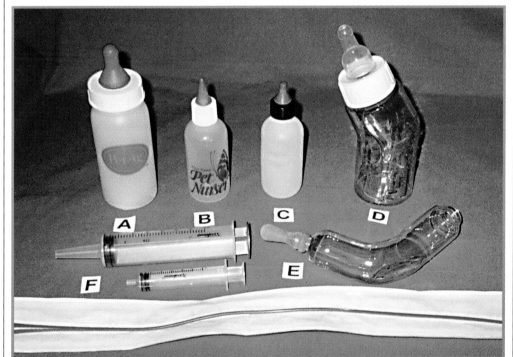

If you choose to handfeed your puppies you will need to invest in the proper equipment, such as bottles, syringes, and a feeding tube.

diarrhea develops, or add a few drops if constipation develops.

METHODS OF HANDFEEDING

   There are two basic methods of feeding newborn puppies: bottle feeding and tube feeding. The latter is riskier but is the best choice for weak puppies that have feeble nursing reflexes. Bottle feeding satisfies the normal

stimulation. It also takes a great deal of time if there are more than one or two puppies to feed.

Weighing the Puppy

   Whatever method you use, be sure to weigh the puppy daily for the first two weeks, and at least weekly thereafter, to ensure proper weight gain. Newborns will normally lose a little weight the

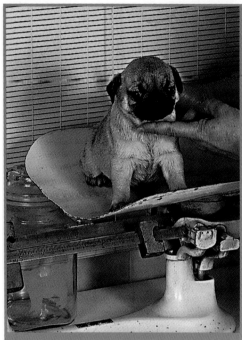

It is important to weigh all newborn puppies daily to check that they are gaining weight properly.

seriously and the cause investigated. Perhaps the formula is not rich enough or the amount is inadequate. Maybe the puppy has a heavy worm infestation that is robbing him of nutrients. Many puppies are born with roundworms, and all should have a stool sample checked early because worming, with veterinary recommendation, can be done as young as four weeks of age. "Failure to thrive" is a generic term for puppies that fail to gain weight and muscle tone for no obvious reason. Sometimes this weak condition is caused by digestive system or metabolic malfunctions, virus or bacterial infections, or congenital deformities.

first day or two, but after that there should be a steady increase. Normal puppies should gain about one to two grams (0.035 to 0.07 ounce) *per day* for each pound of anticipated adult weight. This translates to about 10 to 20 grams (0.5 ounce) per day for a small breed under 15 pounds adult weight, and to about 100 to 200 grams (3.5 to 7 ounces) for a giant breed over 100 pounds adult weight. The general "rule of thumb" is that a newborn puppy should double its weight in eight to ten days.

Although weight gain slows proportionately as the puppy grows so that the gain relative to his current weight will be less in a six-week-old than in a younger puppy, any failure to gain over several days should be taken

It is important to remember that any puppy that does not sufficiently gain weight or shows signs of illness should be brought to the veterinarian's attention.

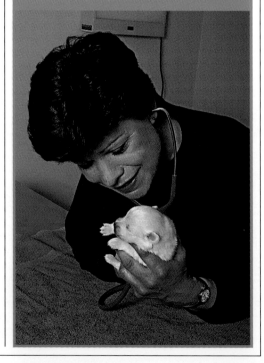

Tube Feeding

The equipment needed for tube feeding is a soft rubber French infant feeding tube, #8 for small breeds and #10 for large breeds, and a 12 cc to 20 cc syringe, both of which can be obtained from veterinarians or pharmacies.

The great danger with tube feeding is passing the tube into the lungs instead of the stomach. If formula is pushed into a esophagus. *Remember to re-mark the distance as the puppy grows.*

You can test if the tube is inserted properly in the esophagus by placing the end of the inserted tube in a container of water to see if any bubbles of air are coming from the tube. If the tube is pushed into the trachea of a normal puppy, it will struggle and cough, but a weak puppy might not react.

The tip of a correctly measured feeding tube should reach almost to the last rib of the puppy.

neonatal's lungs, there is basically nothing that can be done except watch him die from drowning or humanely euthanize him. To avoid this, mark the tube with a piece of tape or an indelible marker at a long enough length that the tip reaches almost to the last rib. This prevents mistakes, because if the tube enters the trachea instead of the esophagus, it will be stopped short of the marked distance because the trachea is much shorter than the

Before you pick up the puppy, the amount calculated for one feeding should be drawn up into the syringe. Turn the syringe up to the ceiling and push out any air that may have entered the syringe. Injecting air with the formula can cause colic. The formula should be near body temperature, or about 90 degrees Fahrenheit, otherwise it could shock the puppy's stomach because it has not been warmed by its passage down the esophagus.

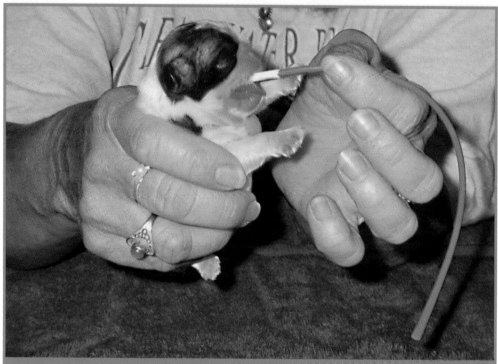

A correctly inserted feeding tube will not cause a puppy any undue discomfort.

If you think there might be any delay before the feeding, place the filled syringe in a container of body temperature water to keep it warm while you get ready. Water will not enter the syringe unless the plunger is pulled back. The same container of water can be used to test the tube placement.

If the air temperature is below 75 degrees Fahrenheit, wrap the puppy loosely in a cloth when you remove him from his bed to prevent chilling. With the filled syringe waiting, hold the puppy with the nondominant hand (hereafter termed "left" for convenience; left-handed caretakers translate to "right") either on a table or your lap, with his stomach down. Place your left thumb and forefinger

against the cheeks on either side of the puppy's mouth and apply gentle pressure until the mouth opens. If this does not open the mouth, use the little finger of the hand holding the tube to gently pry open the jaws. By keeping a little pressure on the cheeks, the mouth can then easily be held open.

Insert the tube into the mouth, over the tongue, and *slowly* push the tube in until you hit the mark. In newborn puppies the tube usually goes down effortlessly. *Do not force the tube.* Now slip your fingers from the cheeks to hold the tube in place. If you are not sure of the tube's placement because the tube seemed difficult to insert or because it stopped short of your mark, now is the time to check for proper insertion by dipping the tube opening into water and watching for bubbles.

If all seems well, use your right hand to attach the syringe to the tube and *slowly* push the plunger with your thumb (fingers are around the syringe). Holding the syringe in this manner gives you the best control of the plunger.

firmly and ignore this protest.

Remove the tube without drawing back on or unhooking the syringe.

Flush the tube and syringe with hot soapy water, rinse everything several times, and store the tube and separated syringe and plunger in a covered, dry place. The so-called "disposable" syringes can be washed and

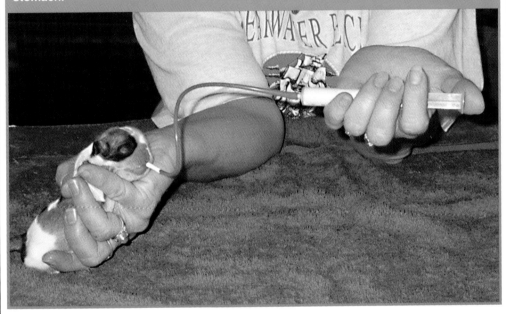

Be sure the flow of formula is controlled and that no air is injected into the puppy's stomach.

When you are comfortable with tube feeding, you can have the syringe already attached to the tube before inserting it. In this case, before you begin inserting the tube, push the plunger just enough to fill the tube with formula, letting one or two drops fall out. This eliminates all air. As the puppy gets stronger, he may struggle or try to "complain" when the formula is injected, but as long as you are sure of the positioning, just hold

reused many times, usually for as long as a puppy will be tube fed. If you wish, boil them for five minutes to sterilize them after the day's last feeding, but it is not necessary to do so long as they are washed well. If the plunger on the syringe starts to stick, apply a drop of cooking oil for lubrication, being sure to wipe off any excess.

Bottle Feeding

There can be two problems with bottle feeding. One is that

newborns often have a low nursing drive and are slow to suck effectively, especially on an artificial nipple. It may take several minutes for a neonate to ingest the required amount of formula, so if time is a critical factor, tube feed your pups. Perhaps you can let the puppy nurse for a while to get the practice, then tube feed the remainder of the formula, or let the puppy nurse for one or two feedings a day when time is not critical. After the first few days, the puppy will become more efficient.

The other problem is finding the right nipple for your puppy. Most newborn puppies are too small to use human nipples, but a nipple made especially for premature babies will suit medium- to large-breed puppies. Check with your local pharmacy or hospital as several styles and sizes are available. Pick a nipple that is as narrow and long as possible and that has a soft, highly flexible texture. The nipples that come with most nursing sets commonly sold for pets are useful for small breeds or for larger breed puppies under two weeks old.

The hole in the nipple will probably have to be made larger by piercing it with a heated needle or cutting a small X with a razor blade. When the bottle is turned upside down, the formula should

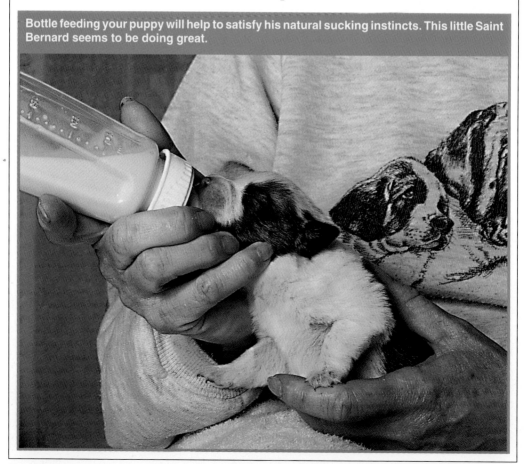

Bottle feeding your puppy will help to satisfy his natural sucking instincts. This little Saint Bernard seems to be doing great.

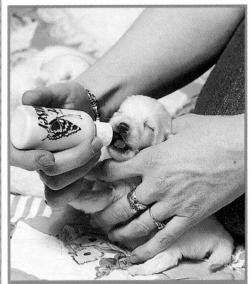
The size of the nipple you choose is very important to your puppy's success with bottle feeding.

touching his mouth, he should begin to swing his head back and forth. This is an instinctive movement that searches for the nipple. It sometimes fails to lead to the puppy taking hold of the nipple at first, because the nipples we use are not very natural to the puppy and may not trigger the instinctual behavior. If you make sure the nipple is warmed to formula temperature by holding the bottle upside down for a few seconds before starting to feed, and then squeeze a little formula onto the tip, puppies will sometimes take to it right away. If not, you will have to apply a little pressure against the sides of the puppy's mouth to open it and slip

very slowly bead up and drip from the nipple without any pressure being applied. A hole that is too small will discourage and tire the pup, so that he is apt to quit nursing before he receives adequate nutrition. A hole that is too large can cause the puppy to choke and aspirate formula, a prelude to pneumonia.

The easiest position to bottle feed is with the puppy resting in your lap or on a table in front of you. Be sure there is a non-slip surface under the puppy, such as a towel, because when a puppy really "gets into" nursing, he pushes backward with his hind feet for leverage. Hold the puppy with your left hand, put your thumb and forefinger under the edge of the puppy's jaw bone to hold the head still while the other fingers cradle the body, and press the nipple to the puppy's lips.

When the puppy feels the nipple

With a little practice, your puppy will be eagerly sucking from a bottle in no time!

the nipple in. Often puppies will attempt to get this foreign object out of their mouth, so you must cradle the head in your left fingers to prevent this.

Practice with the bottle held in nursing position before you begin feeding and learn how much pressure you must use to get a couple of drops of formula at a time out of the nipple. Once you have the nipple in the puppy's mouth, squeeze a couple of drops out. This will often stimulate nursing in a reluctant puppy. Be careful not to express too much at a time, or the puppy may choke or perhaps breathe in the formula. This squeezing tactic may have to be repeated many times as the puppy learns to nurse and gains strength. If after a couple of sessions, the pup has not caught on and is still not nursing strongly, try a different shape or texture of nipple. Wiggle the bottle a little if the pup seems to be falling asleep while nursing. Sometimes gently pulling the nipple out half way will cause the pup to renew sucking efforts. Getting a pup started sometimes requires a bit of patience, but is well worth the trouble in order to allow him the most natural experience possible.

Once the puppy is a few days old, it will want to "pad" or "knead" with his front feet as he nurses. By placing the flat of your left hand toward the puppy underneath the bottle, you can

Got milk? This little Pug proudly displays his milk mustache.

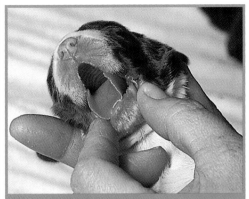

"Okay, okay, I'm ready." At first it may be necessary to guide your puppy toward the nipple.

provide a surface for this instinctive behavior. Some bottle tops are wide enough for the puppy to put his feet on.

If you have a very strong puppy that pushes hard with his hind feet and gets excited about the bottle, you may have to use your left hand to keep the pup safely in place. In this case, hold the bottle with only your thumb and forefinger of your right hand, and turn the palm of this hand toward the puppy to provide a place for his front feet. Some pups nurse so hard that they arch their backs and lift their bodies off the surface. If you have such an eager puppy, just give him some gentle support under his body and use

your right palm as above for the front feet to press against. If you are feeding large-breed puppies, you may need to wear a glove on the bottle-holding hand to prevent scratches, especially if it is a large litter.

Sometimes eager puppies get a little frantic when they smell and feel the nipple and they continually overcompensate with their head swings, missing the nipple. If this happens, hold the bottle in just your forefinger and thumb, and cup the rest of your hand around in a half circle making a guide for the head. Once the pup has the nipple, keep your fingers cradled around the head so that he will not lose it again in his active nursing.

After each feeding, the bottle, nipple, and rim should be separated and washed in dish detergent, then thoroughly rinsed and air-dried, with the opening placed down on an absorbent surface such as a clean paper towel. If desired, they may be sterilized according to manufacturer instructions.

Amount to Feed

Table 2 shows "Age in Weeks" and the estimated amount of formula to feed per day in milliliters (ml), which is the same as the cubic centimeter (cc) markings on syringes for every 100 grams (gm) of puppy weight. One regular teaspoon contains 5 ml. This amount is only an estimate and individual puppy requirements may differ depending upon the breed and the environment. *You must weigh*

Table 2 illustrates the proper amount of formula your puppy should receive according to his age.

Estimated Amount to Feed	
Age (weeks) / Amount to Feed **per 100 gm Weight**	
1	13ml
2	17ml
3	20ml
4	22ml

Monitoring the weight of your puppy will help you to regulate the amount of formula he is given.

the puppy regularly to be sure it is gaining weight on the amount you are feeding.

Many veterinarians and breeders handfeed every two hours around the clock for the first week. However, there is no scientific proof that feedings for healthy puppies need to be that frequent and most puppies will do well on fewer feedings. Consult your veterinarian and then decide what schedule is best for your circumstances.

For most puppies, the amount to be given per day can be divided into six feedings for the first two or three weeks, then into four feedings per day until weaning. For example, if the first feeding on a four-feeding schedule is at seven in the morning, when you get up, and the last is to be just before you go to bed at ten at night, then feedings should be at about 7 am, 12 noon, 5 pm, and 10 pm. For a couple of weeks, the pup may wake during the night and need an extra feeding, just like a human infant.

STIMULATING ELIMINATION

Puppies younger than three weeks of age require stimulation to eliminate. Without external stimulation, a puppy can become impacted or toxic due to retained wastes. Stimulation can be provided by using a cotton ball or soft cloth dipped in warm water to massage the genital area several times a day. Most handraisers do this right after feeding a puppy. After three weeks of age this can

An orphaned puppy will have to rely on you for the grooming and stimulation his dam and littermates would have provided.

This little Golden puppy exhibits instinctive behavior as he kneads with his front paws while eagerly nursing.

be discontinued, although you must still clean the area daily if the dam is not attending to the puppies. See the chapter dealing with sick puppies if the stool is not pale brown and semiformed or if the urine is orange or thick like honey. Puppies often swallow air with the formula and should be "burped" by gentle patting and rubbing on the back after each feeding, just like human babies.

SUMMARY

This outline reviews the essentials of the foster rearing program so that you can get a quick overview to remind you of the steps until you know the routine.

Temperature

90 degrees Fahrenheit, days 1-5.
85 degrees Fahrenheit, days 6-10.
Decrease to 75 degrees Fahrenheit at 28 days and hold there to six weeks of age.

Feeding

Newborn: feed six times daily, formula warmed to about 90 degrees Fahrenheit. Burp and stimulate elimination after each feeding. Add solids at 21 days—wean at 28 days.

Comfort Care

Massage briefly before each feeding. Apply baby oil if skin is dry. Prevent drafts. Separate puppies to prevent suckling.

Disease

Immunize according to veterinarian recommendation. Wash hands after petting strange dogs. Check for signs of illness, sores, etc.

WEANING

When you are ready to begin weaning to a dish, add a little extra to the amount that you were handfeeding because for the first few feedings, some will surely be spilled or smeared onto the pup's coat. When you start adding solids to the formula, feed what the puppy will clean up at each meal, plus a little left over. That way you can be assured he is getting enough—but watch the pup's weight! As the pup grows, he will naturally need a larger volume of food. The amount to be fed should be determined by the puppy. He should eat enough to maintain a steady weight gain, but not so much that he becomes obese and has trouble running and playing. Puppies will normally eat about one and a half times as much of a given food as adult dogs of the same general size. For example, a 30-pound, four-month-old dog will eat at least as much as a 45-pound adult.

A puppy will start to lap from a shallow dish held under his chin as soon as he can sit up steadily, usually around two weeks of age, but it is not advisable to feed this way at that early age unless there is no other choice. The pup is not very coordinated at this stage, and the sneeze reflex is weak, so the puppy could breathe in formula if his head dips into the

Puppies grow very quickly and require especially nutritious meals to develop into healthy adults.

Your puppy will need help when being introduced to eating formula from a dish. This two-week-old Springer Spaniel seems to be getting the hang of it.

milk. It is better to wait until three or four weeks of age before the pup feeds himself.

The first attempts at dish feeding should be with the puppy's regular formula placed in a saucer and held at a comfortable height in front of the puppy. If you try to make him lap from a dish on the floor his first few tries, the puppy will undoubtedly fall into the dish, splash around, and generally make a mess. Then you will not be able to determine just how much formula actually got into the stomach. After the pup has gotten the idea and developed a little skill, the formula can be placed in a straight-sided, non-tip dish, such as a heavy crock or individual casserole dish, for self-feeding.

A special puppy food dish made of stainless steel with a raised center section to keep the puppies out of the food can be purchased, or such a dish can be improvised. Try placing a bowl slightly smaller than the food dish upside down in the center of the dish so that the food is confined to a narrow space around the edge, or put some heavy solid object, such as a smooth, clean rock, in the dish. This prevents the puppy from sliding into the food when he puts his front feet in the dish. If you have two or more small-breed puppies to wean, try putting their food into sections of a muffin tin.

At this point, the formula can be thickened by adding one of the following—baby pabulum cereal (high protein or mixed grain types are good), thoroughly soaked and mashed puppy kibble, or a small amount of canned puppy food. Gradually increase the amount of solids at each meal until the food is semisolid like thick oatmeal. At the end of one week of transition, the pup should be able to handle regular softened puppy food. If the puppy gets smeared with food, be sure to wash it off immediately after the meal with a warm wet cloth because dried puppy gruel, with its high starch content, is like glue on the coat and must later be soaked to soften it before

Are these two puppies going to cooking class? Muffin pans can be used to feed small puppies like these five-week-old Chihuahuas.

The transition between formula and solid food should be gradual. Increase the amount of solids at each meal until the food is semisolid like thick oatmeal.

cultures of *Lactobacillus acidophilus*" does not appear, then there would be no benefit in feeding it. Live cultures of beneficial bacteria are also useful to aid digestion and absorption of nutrients whenever your dog is under stress or receiving antibiotic therapy and may be given to newborns to afford their digestive system a good start.

Remember that after weaning, the puppy needs a constant supply of clean water. Use a non-tip shallow dish, one that is attached to the side of the puppy box or one that is braced in a corner with objects the puppy cannot move, to prevent spills that could promote chilling. Prolonged dampness in the caretaker's absence can create a dangerous bacterial bloom.

it can be scraped off. If left on the hair, dried food can promote bacterial skin infections and irritation.

The slow transition to solid food is important because the puppy's digestive enzymes and intestinal flora need time to adjust to the various food ingredients. This adjustment can be assisted by supplying either a commercially prepared *Lactobacillus* medium, which usually comes in gel form in a tube and is available in most pet supply stores or through catalogs or by adding a teaspoon of plain yogurt that contains live cultures to each meal. If you choose to add the fresh yogurt, read the label to be sure the product contains live cultures. If the statement, "contains live

This little guy must be really thirsty! It is important to provide your puppy with cool, clean water at all times.

FOOD CHOICE

For large breeds of dogs, the most practical food for most owners is kibble, as they would have to feed several cans of food a day. Even for small breeds, kibble is the healthiest choice for normal dogs because it contains all the nutrients found in canned food, minus the water, which you can have to do in order to properly digest the kibble, they might increase their likelihood of suffering from bloat, a life-threatening condition. Even as adults these dogs should be fed two small meals daily rather than one large one and should not be exercised for at least an hour after feeding.

During your puppy's transition to solid food it is important to provide him with a small amount of live cultures daily to aid in digestion and nutrient absorption.

add back in if you choose. If fed only partially soaked or dry, kibble also provides some tooth and gum exercise.

Large- and giant-breed puppies and adolescents should be fed kibble partially or totally presoaked with warm water. If they eat a large bowl of dry kibble and then drink water, which they

Small breeds require concentrated nutrients because their metabolism is higher than that of their larger cousins, so a high-quality, premium kibble is the best choice. If you have a toy breed, ask your veterinarian about hypoglycemia. Be familiar with the symptoms and treatment, as toy breed puppies

A healthy puppy will look forward to mealtime. It seems like this little guy can't wait!

and adults when under stress sometimes develop low blood sugar and will "faint." This is distressing and can be life threatening if not treated, but treatment is simple, and once you are aware of the circumstances that your pet finds stressful, you can be prepared.

Whatever food you intend to feed to the adult dog should be used for the final stages of weaning. Once your dog is used to a certain type and brand of food, do not change without good reason. Contrary to the human-oriented advertisements, your dog does not crave any variety unless you condition him to expect it, and once your dog's system is adjusted to a particular diet it will do best if maintained on it indefinitely. If it becomes

necessary to switch because your dog does not seem to be doing well on a particular food or it is no longer available, be sure to change over gradually, replacing no more than one-fourth of the volume of the previous food with the new at each feeding. If the transition is too abrupt, a digestive upset can occur, and the result will be diarrhea. If this happens, stop offering the new food at once, reintroduce it more slowly, or follow the advice of your veterinarian.

FEEDING SCHEDULES

Once the puppy is eating solid food there are two general methods of feeding. One is "free choice" or "ad lib" feeding, which

Consult a breeder or your veterinarian about the appropriate diet for your puppies.

It is important to feed your puppies a well-balanced diet in order to keep them healthy and happy.

is popular with large kennels because it reduces labor. The daily ration of dry kibble is either measured once daily into feeding dishes or large weatherproof containers are filled with several days' worth at a time. The dogs eat at their leisure. The drawbacks to this method are that many dogs, especially puppies, will overeat, becoming obese, and if you take your dog with you on trips, keeping food available all day is problematical.

The second, more popular method is "limited" or "timed" feeding. Feed as much as the puppy wants to consume in a given period of time—20 minutes is usually long enough—and then remove the dish and discard or cover and refrigerate leftovers. Timed feeding promotes good food habits in the puppy, avoids the possibility of spoiled food, and is the way most breeders feed their puppies. Any healthy puppy will eat all he needs in just a few minutes, and if he learns the dish will be removed soon, he will get down to business and not play with the food as much.

NUMBER OF FEEDINGS

Puppies from four to eight weeks of age can be fed three or four times a day, with four being the number most breeders use. This allows the daily ration to be offered in smaller amounts that the puppy can digest more easily. From 8 to 12 weeks of age, three meals a day can be fed, and from 4 months to 8 months (for small breeds) or 12 months (for large breeds) two meals daily are appropriate. Adult dogs do well on either one or two feedings daily.

SPECIAL NEEDS OF SINGLE PUPPIES

PROPS AND FURNITURE

Newborn puppies have an instinct to "cuddle." They feel most secure when they are surrounded closely by objects, which, of course, under average circumstances would be littermates and the dam's body. To provide this security for a single puppy, tightly roll towels or other soft materials and bind with masking tape or shoestrings, etc. For smaller puppies, cotton tube or crew socks can be filled with clean rags or anything washable. Place them on three sides of the pup, preferably in a location such as a corner, where the pup can push against them without moving them around. You will see that the pup presses himself up to these props, in a few days often climbing halfway over so that his head can hang down the other side as he sleeps contentedly. Puppies seem to especially like

This two-week-old Springer Spaniel seems perfectly cozy with his cuddling substitute.

Newborn puppies have an instinctive need to cuddle and without their mother and littermates, they need to be provided with substitutes. Rolled simulated sheepskin, a rolled towel, or a stuffed sock work well.

being crammed tightly between two props. If you want to use stuffed toys, be sure they are made of nonshedding material with nontoxic dyes. Artificial sheepskin pads, such as those used in hospitals to prevent bedsores and that can now be found in many pet supply stores, or stuffed toys made from this material, make excellent props. When single newborn pups are provided with this psychological "furniture," they seem to become more profoundly relaxed and easily enter active sleep. Uncomfortable or insecure puppies wake easily, tend to whimper, and spend a lot of time rooting around.

A healthy, contented pup will sleep deeply, twitching and jerking. These actions indicate that connections are being strengthened in the puppy's system and nerves and muscles are learning to coordinate.

It is important to a young puppy's normal development to be handled regularly.

PHYSIOLOGICAL STIMULATION

Several articles I have read on neonatal puppy care advise something like the following: "All newborn puppies should be kept as free as possible from any disturbance or handling." It is true that newborns should not be handled excessively, meaning with such frequency that the pup is not getting adequate deep rest. However, the term "as free as possible" could easily be misinterpreted as calling for the *opposite* extreme of handling only the minimum necessary for feeding and elimination. Too little physical stimulation is as harmful as too much. When a pup is in a normal litter that is being cared for by the dam, he is frequently rolled around, pushed, climbed on, and licked all over. He must compete for food by pushing, shoving, crawling, and learning to stay attached to the nipple. This is healthy exercise and a necessary part of physical learning. It promotes nerve and muscle growth and lays the foundation for the coordinated movements needed for walking.

If you are handraising a single puppy, you must provide this needed stimulation. Gently rolling the puppy around and massaging him with your fingers is excellent puppy stimulation. Do this for a couple of minutes before each feeding. If you are bottle feeding, gently pull the nipple away from the pup a few times during each feeding. Get him to strain a little at keeping his suction (see feeding section for more techniques). Make him "fight" a little for his food. In between feedings, pass by once in awhile and just give the pup a gentle little push or rub. Disturb him just as a littermate would, so he responds with some small sound or movement, but not enough to totally arouse him. Another way to provide gentle physiological stimulation is to buy or make a puppy carrypack and carry the pup around while you work around the home. The pack should hold the puppy against your chest and be anchored with straps attached to the bottom of the pouch so it will not swing out when you bend forward. The sound of your heartbeat, your strong scent, and the subtle motions caused by your changes of position provide both psychological comfort and stimulation for nerve development.

PSYCHOLOGICAL AND SOCIAL ENVIRONMENT

Substitute Siblings

As an aid to teaching a single puppy social skills, you should have a model substitute sibling (SS for short) a brother or sister in the form of a stuffed toy or filled socks put together to form a generalized dog form. The eyes, nose, and mouth should be prominent on this model so that the puppy can easily see them with his poor eyesight. These features are best formed by using embroidery, indelible markers, or cloth cutouts that are firmly sewn on. The button-type eyes and noses can come off and get swallowed by a pup and may result either in choking or an intestinal blockage. The model's body should be of a washable material. It does not matter if the model has "fur," but if you prefer a soft, cuddly SS, the imitation lamb's wool type is suitable. Just make sure the fur does not come out when pulled on, or the pup will end up ingesting too many fibers. Size is not of major importance, but for the average size puppy (using 35–45 pounds adult weight as an average), the SS body should be smaller than a bread box and a little bigger than four fists put together. A more complete mimicking is possible if the SS's ears and tail can be held in up and down positions. If the ears and tail are soft, a flexible wire can be inserted around the edges of the ears and into the tail, but be sure the ends of the wire are not able to poke the puppy. To prevent any possible injury, do not leave the wired SS with an unsupervised puppy. If possible, scent the SS by rubbing a damp cloth onto a healthy dog unknown to the puppy, especially around his mouth and ears where the dog's scent is strong, and then onto the SS. If there will be a long delay between collecting the scent and presenting the SS to the puppy, seal the scented cloth in a plastic bag and apply the scent to the SS just before the socialization session. The use of the SS with a single puppy is discussed below for each stage of puppy development. A model SS is also a useful aid for modifying the social behavior of any overly dominant or submissive puppy. This use is discussed in the section on teaching social limits.

STAGES OF DEVELOPMENT

Puppies go through several distinct stages of behavioral development. These are, according

This little puppy seems thrilled to meet his substitute sibling.

to the original research by J. P. Scott and J. L. Fuller that is detailed in the book *Genetics and the Social Behavior of Dogs*:
(1) Neonatal: birth to 2 weeks;
(2) Transitional: 2 to 3 weeks;
(3) Socialization: 3 to 12 weeks;
(4) Juvenile: 12 weeks to 6 months or later. Within this general framework are defined periods that are termed *critical periods*. Knowledge of these stages are important for everyone raising puppies, and vital to those who must provide for single puppies.

Neonatal: Birth to Two Weeks

During this stage, the puppy is blind, deaf, and has practically no sense of smell. The most highly developed senses are touch, taste, balance, or response to gravity

The neonatal puppy is born blind and deaf and needs little more than a full belly and cozy surroundings for the first two weeks of life.

(the pup will immediately struggle to turn over if turned on his back and yelp in distress if parts of its body are unsupported), and negative response (withdrawal) to cold or extreme heat. The only locomotion is a slow crawl forward accomplished mainly by using the front legs. Only the nerves that serve the mouth and jaws and the sense of balance are completely developed. The characteristic vocalization is a distress yelp given when the pup is cold or in pain. The brain itself is still mostly undeveloped. There are only a few convolutions in the cortex (the outermost layer of the brain, commonly called the "gray matter") that indicates a greatly reduced learning ability compared to the adult form of cortex. The pup at this age even needs stimulation to begin feeding and newborns that are warm and secure will lie quietly for many hours showing no hunger distress. When he is disturbed enough, the puppy will begin to move around, swinging his head back and forth searching for a nipple.

There are no social capacities during this stage so SS interactions are not needed. Brain waves at this age are minimal and show no difference between waking and sleeping states.

Transitional: Two to Three Weeks

This period begins when the puppy's eyes are completely open, usually around 13 days of age. A puppy this age will readily nurse from a bottle and can even lap in a poorly coordinated fashion from a dish held under his chin. By three weeks most puppies are coordinated enough to eat from a dish on their own, although the process can be very messy, and weaning to semisolid food can begin. In the wild, canine mothers start regurgitating partly digested food for their puppies when they are about three to four weeks old.

While in the neonatal period, vocalizations were given only in response to cold or pain. Now puppies begin to wander around and yelp when left alone in a strange environment, showing increased awareness of "place." Brain waves at three weeks begin to display higher amplitudes and the patterns of sleeping and wakeful states are differentiated. Although the part of the brain devoted to vision shows activity as soon as the eyes open, the puppy is probably not fully capable of observing forms until about four weeks of age and does not have adult vision capacity until after eight weeks. At about 20 days of age, the startle response to sound becomes apparent as the ear canals open.

Also at about 20 days, the first teeth, the incisors, usually begin pushing through the gums. When this occurs, puppies will start to bite and chew in addition to sucking and licking. After three weeks, puppies begin to interact socially, with clumsy attempts at play fighting, and as they are now able to walk, they will move from the nest to eliminate. This is when a divided puppy box is useful to begin clean habits and when you should begin acting as substitute

As your puppy begins to grow, he will need increased interaction to stimulate his normal development.

sibling for the single puppy.

At this age, all you need to do is push the puppy with the front of the SS until it "fights" back and mouths the SS. Do this for a couple minutes before each feeding, and then leave the SS with the puppy when he sleeps.

Socialization: Three to Twelve Weeks

Now the caregiver for a single puppy must pay special attention to the social needs of the pup. If the dam is feeding and interacting with the puppy, the need for social stimulation is less urgent but not eliminated, as the pup interacts differently with his mother than with his siblings. Even if the dam is one of those gems of motherhood that likes to spend a lot of time interacting with her baby, the pup will always be submissive to her. It needs practice at being both dominant and submissive with other dogs, and this is the period of development during which primary social skills are learned. If social learning is prevented at this age, the puppy will never have the stable social character he could have had, for it is not something that can be totally overcome by later learning.

At three weeks of age, puppies in a litter move around independently from one another, but by five weeks they will be moving as a group, for instance, to greet a human. This is the beginning of pack behavior. During this period, fear reactions begin to develop. At about five weeks of age, puppies will begin to startle and cringe away from any loud noise or sudden movement and may become fearful of unfamiliar humans. However, if they are handled, this puppy fear will disappear within two weeks. The fear reaction to new things in the environment appears at the same time that the pup starts to explore his surroundings, and in wild dogs this "fear everything unknown and approach with caution" attitude is a survival mechanism. A three-week-old will stay near the den, but by six weeks of age, a puppy will begin to explore farther and farther from the den.

For house-raised pups, this period of gradual environmental learning may be accelerated. Carry the puppy about or encourage him to follow the caregiver so that he is rapidly familiarized with a wide area. Things that have been a consistent part of the puppy's environment throughout this period, such as vacuum cleaners and visitors, will not trigger this fear response. Puppies in this critical period between 4 and 12 weeks of age should be introduced to new things slowly and with encouragement. Moral support in the form of a constant light touch and low-pitched, quiet words will reassure the puppy and give him the courage to approach and explore novel stimuli.

TEACHING SOCIAL SKILLS USING A SUBSTITUE SIBLING

By seven weeks of age, play fighting has evolved into true dominance interactions. The single-puppy caregiver should now spend several minutes each day using the SS to interact with the pup. Dogs communicate with stereotyped expressions and body postures in addition to sounds. Although facial movements cannot be displayed, an SS can be used to mimic gross body postures and illicit typical dog behavior from a puppy. The person animating the SS can growl and press the SS to the pup's shoulder area to mimic domination. Sometimes the SS should be backed away when the pup responds with a growl, the SS's rear turned submissively toward the pup. Sometimes the SS should be pressed harder toward the puppy until he is held down by the "dominant" SS and "gives up" with a whimper or exhibits escape behavior.

Play behavior is mimicked by facing the SS toward the pup and play soliciting by bowing the SS down or bouncing it rapidly back and forth, then running it away when the pup charges, turning it back to rush at the puppy in a second or two. Through these types of interactions the puppy can experience being both

puppy can be taught to control himself. If he never learns this lesson he can become hard-mouthed, a behavior in which a threat or play bite can result in unintended injury.

When a puppy or dog nibbles rapidly with his front teeth on another, it is called epimeletic behavior and is a pleasure

At only three weeks of age, puppies will begin to interact socially, clumsily play fighting and grooming each other.

dominant and submissive and can practice playful role reversal, learning what play signals mean.

During this stage puppies learn to inhibit their bite. If they bite a littermate too hard, it responds with a yelp and escapes, ending the play, and the biter soon learns to be careful of his teeth. A single pup must be taught this by the caregiver. Many breeders forbid mouthing by their puppies, but in general, this is a mistake. By allowing gentle mouth play and then acting "hurt" by yelping, "No!" and withdrawing the hand when the bites are too hard, the

response or bonding ritual. This "grooming" can cause the receiver's skin to be pinched painfully but should not be punished. Just gently redirect the pup's attention to something else.

The command "easy" can be taught in conjunction with the above exercises. As the pup begins to mouth you quietly say, "Easy" each time the bite pressure is a little strong. If the warning is not heeded, stop the play and close your hand snugly around the pup's muzzle for a second (mimicking a muzzle hold by another dog) and repeat the command. Then allow him to take your hand in his mouth again. If this lesson is repeated frequently, the pup will learn that this command means to control himself and then the command can later be easily transferred to roughhousing or too-exuberant play in general.

LIVE SUBSTITUTE SIBLINGS

If the dam of a single puppy is not the playful type or the pup is an orphan, a live SS should be brought in to play with the pup if at all possible, just as soon as the puppy has received his last immunization. Of course, if you have another dog that is not traveling off your property where he could

It is important to afford your puppy plenty of opportunity to associate with other animals and people. These two English Springer Spaniel pups enjoy the company of their young friend.

pick up diseases and that seems to be a good "pup-sitter" candidate, he can be introduced to the pup at four weeks of age and act as full-time SS, saving you much interaction time. If not, perhaps a friend or neighbor has a healthy and well-groomed puppy or dog that can come for visits. The visiting dog should not be so large that it will overwhelm the puppy, so uncontrolled or exuberant that it will kill the pup with kindness, nor so much smaller than the pup that the puppy, in his social ignorance, might hurt the visitor and cause him to react defensively.

Make the first introduction with the pup in your hands or lap and the SS on a leash, controlled by another handler. Let them look briefly at each other, then turn the puppy's rear toward the stranger so it can sniff the pup's anal area until it is satisfied. Then have the SS handler turn it around and reverse the procedure. This is the natural way dogs introduce each other in a non-threatening manner. The SS should be kept on leash until the initial excitement is over and you can be sure the stranger will not be too rough with the baby. Expect some hesitancy on both their parts until they are sure of each other and some yelps and growls when the play gets going. Be alert, do not leave them unattended, but also do not be overprotective. Healthy puppies

A pup's personality will often be evident in the way he interacts with other puppies. These two compete for "top dog."

are very resilient and pliable. Noisy roughhouse squabbling happens with all puppies.

This 3 to 12 week period is the most important critical period in the dog's life. Its experiences during this time will determine what species the dog will accept as "relatives" when he is adult. If the pup is not socialized to other dogs by 12 weeks of age, he will identify too strongly with humans and will pay little attention to his own kind. This lack of same-species social identification can be a problem in a male dog that is to be part of a breeding program.

The human-raised pup, or a pup removed from his litter before eight weeks of age and not socialized with other dogs, can fail to develop normal sexual behavior, orienting his instinctive drive exclusively toward humans, a behavior that can be extremely annoying in a male pet. A puppy left totally unhandled until 12 weeks of age will react to humans like a wild animal. It will have to be "tamed" and will never form strong bonds with humans other than his caretaker because he will retain the wild fear response to unfamiliar people.

ENVIRONMENTAL ENRICHMENT

Sometime around three weeks of age the puppy will begin to show interest in his environment. An assortment of toys should be provided in and out of the box or sleeping area. At this young age, toys need not be "tough" because the puppy has not learned to chew hard yet. Cardboard toilet paper and paper towel rolls, small stuffed toys, latex toys with interestingly textured surfaces, and balls small enough for the pup to get his mouth over are good choices. A "ball" for young puppies can be fashioned out of a rolled-up piece of material, such as a washcloth, and fastened with adhesive tape. Use your imagination to turn everyday objects into toys, making sure that there are no removable parts small enough to become stuck in the puppy's throat and no loose strings for the pup to get tangled up in. Be especially careful that the squeakers in any toys are of the molded-in type and cannot become detached because these are the perfect size to enter a puppy's airway. Puppies will ingest fraying material and could develop an intestinal blockage, so throw out any toys that begin to unravel.

At six weeks of age, puppies begin to chew harder as their rear molar teeth come in. Nylabones®

As your puppy becomes more aware of his environment, be sure to provide him with plenty of fun and safe toys to play with. This young Pug enjoys a romp with his favorite ball.

POPpups™ are healthy treats for your puppy. When bone-hard they help to control plaque build-up; when microwaved they become a rich cracker which your pup will love. The POPpup™ is available in liver and other flavors and is fortified with calcium.

are an excellent toy for this age because they have a texture and flavor attractive to puppies, and give enough resistance to provide chewing satisfaction.

At four weeks of age you can begin to increase the puppy's "IQ," defined here as his healthy curiosity and adaptability, developed through play learning. This age is roughly parallel mentally and emotionally to about six to nine months in a human infant. In both species, their awareness is expanding to include more distant objects, and their urge to explore appears. Now is the time to carefully enrich their environment for long-term benefit to their temperament and emotional stability. If you show the puppy a toy or a piece of food, then hide the object under a cloth or an upside-down box and allow the puppy to "find" it, you can

All of this growing up is hard work! This Rottweiler puppy takes a well-deserved break.

All puppies need to chew! Provide safe and healthy Nylabone® toys, like this Gumabone®, for your puppy's enjoyment.

teach the concept psychologists call "object consistency." The pup learns an out-of-sight object is still there and has not disappeared physically, only visually. This may seem simple, but it requires the subjects of the game to have the ability to maintain a mental image of the object that has disappeared. Introduce novel objects such as balloons or an upside-down flowerpot, anything the pup can safely approach, into the environment as often as possible, and encourage the pup to investigate. Make different noises, such as squeaking into an empty paper towel roll or rattling a can with a coin in it, and praise the pup for approaching and figuring out what the sound is. Most dogs love chasing prey as much as cats do, so tie an old sock or strips of cloth to one end of a long piece of cord and get the puppy to chase it by moving it in a jerky fashion. Exercising the puppy's mind at this impressionable age will help him to grow into a dog that will calmly accept strange objects, people, and events. He will learn that his human leader's judgment about the safety of strange things can be relied upon, laying the foundation for trust.

TEACHING SOCIAL LIMITS THE NATURAL WAY

CORRECTING AGGRESSION

If the puppy displays overly aggressive behavior, such as refusing to acknowledge the SS's submission and continuing to bite or constantly growling and snapping during the play sessions, either with a live or toy SS or person, he must be disciplined by strong growls and a momentary withdrawal of the playmate. If the live SS fails to discipline the pup when he behaves this way, the caretaker should intervene and do so or the puppy may grow into an overly aggressive adult. If the pup refuses to stop the excessive roughness at a growl, pin him to the floor with the toy SS and hold him there until he shows submission by ceasing his struggle, whimpering, wagging his tail, or refusing to make eye contact while his ears and tail are down. This is the same type of correction another dog would give an upstart puppy.

Mounting behavior in puppies and often in adult dogs has no direct connection to sexual behavior. Both males and females will mount another (clasp with the forelegs) to display social dominance, and to the puppy it matters not whether the thing he mounts is a part of a person, a toy, or another animal. Puppies under the age of six months normally do not have the capacity to show true sexual behavior because their hormones have not yet triggered the sex drive. In cases where dominance mounting has become annoying, frequent mounting should be disciplined gently but firmly by saying, "No!" placing the pup in another position, and distracting him with play. If the mounting behavior continues in spite of the consistent use of this redirection over several days, then discipline in the same way as for overly aggressive behavior.

Discipline for overtly aggressive acts, such as too-hard biting with growling or head shaking, should be sharper. Take hold of the skin on the back of the puppy's neck and give it a *slight* shake while saying, "NO!" in a deep, growly voice. As your correction will have

A young puppy will not know the difference between good and bad behavior. It is up to you, the owner, to teach him what is acceptable.

Displays of dominance between puppies are natural and will happen from time to time. Playmates will help each other to learn social limits.

forced him to stop the unwanted behavior, immediately praise and stroke the puppy, drawing a clear line between what is acceptable and what is not. This type of correction mimics the natural lessons a dam gives her puppies.

BUILDING PUPPY CONFIDENCE

If a puppy reacts to SS "rough" play or meeting a person or another dog (toy or not) by giving exaggerated signals of submission, such as lying down and rolling over or urinating, then the caregiver should instill confidence in the pup. The caretaker should let him "win," or be dominant in play more than half of the time. The second the puppy puts his ears or tail up toward the playmate, the SS should back off and play bow. If the puppy rushes at the SS after it has teased the pup by hopping

back and forth, then bowing or turning its rear toward the puppy inviting a chase, the SS should lie down and submit to the puppy. After a few sessions, the puppy's social confidence should be reinforced to a normal level. Another confidence builder is letting the submissive puppy win games of tug-of-war. This form of conditioning should not be indulged in with a dominant, socially outgoing puppy or dog because it can escalate into aggressive displays and give them the illusion that they are in charge.

Puppies of about five weeks of age are starting the stage where they begin to show fear of strange objects, people, and environments. In a wild dog, this is the period in which the home area is imprinted upon the puppy and all of the usual objects in his environment become familiar. The brain is wide open to learning and

Puppies will find mischief whenever possible! Although correction will sometimes be necessary, be sure it is not too harsh.

to forming fears that will last throughout life unless they are counteracted through systematic familiarization. Introduce strange and potentially frightening things carefully to build confidence so that the pup of this age will not be overwhelmed but will learn and explore novel things. In other words, he will "learn to learn" and his mental and emotional development will not be stunted by excessive fear reactions. The ideal response to a novel object is sensible caution, but the puppy should quickly overcome his fear and approach the object, exploring it first with his nose and then with his mouth and feet if the object is non-threatening.

If something, such as a vacuum cleaner, frightens the puppy, encourage him to approach the object (turn any noisy appliance off until the pup gains confidence) by touching the object and the puppy and talking in a soothing monotone, repeating, "It's all right." If the puppy refuses to approach or if the object is large, hold the puppy against your body while you approach the object and maintain contact with it until the pup stops showing signs of distress. Then you touch the puppy's foot to the object while talking soothingly, so the puppy will understand that the object is harmless.

Be sure to have the puppy meet any strangers that happen to visit. If the puppy hangs back but seems interested in this new person, have the visitor sit or squat down and hold out a hand palm up while speaking to the puppy in a happy voice and turning their body at an angle to the puppy. These body signals indicate that the stranger is not a threat. With a hesitant pup, never let the stranger bend over the pup or reach out over his head to pet him, because this can be threatening to the puppy looking up from his low angle and can create a withdrawal response that can become a habit difficult to overcome later.

This drawing demonstrates a substitute sibling in three common stances.

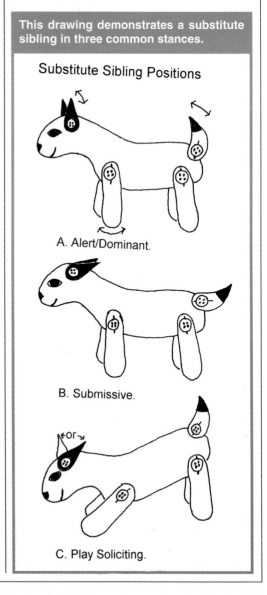

Substitute Sibling Positions

A. Alert/Dominant.

B. Submissive.

C. Play Soliciting.

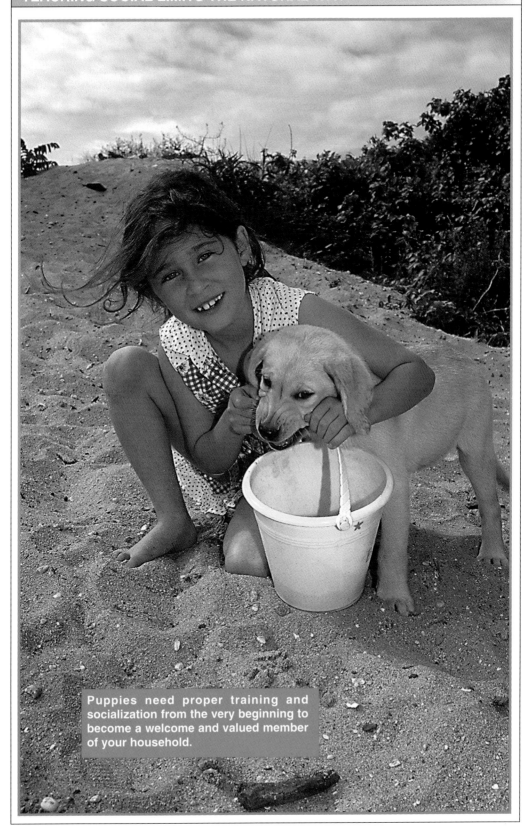

Puppies need proper training and socialization from the very beginning to become a welcome and valued member of your household.

Never punish shyness in any age dog, as that will only make the response worse because punishment increases arousal, reinforcing the fear. Ignore the behavior if it is mild and reward *any* positive reactions—even if the dog just stays still and observes the object of its fear from a distance—by using a happy tone of voice to praise the dog and by gentle caresses. Do not reward shy behavior with physical petting or comfort, as this will reinforce the poor behavior.

Small food treats, which should always be given by the puppy's caretaker or handler and not the stranger (because sometimes this conditions the puppy to "grab" at stranger's hands), can be used to reward the puppy for staying calm

Take your puppy everywhere with you. The more experiences he has, the better socialized he will become!

A lot can be learned about a puppy's behavior and attitude simply by observing his body language.

With the proper supervision, your puppy should be allowed to experience and explore his surroundings.

in the presence of a fear object and to encourage approach. With the puppy on lead, walk him toward the object or person until he begins to show signs of distress, such as a tucked tail, hanging back, etc., then stop and talk to him. When his attention is on the handler and the fear signs disappear, give a food treat and a hearty, "Good Dog!" then take a step or two closer to the object or person. Repeat until the handler and puppy can stand next to the object or person in a relaxed manner. The person should

remain still for the initial training session, and begin to slowly move about only after the puppy is calm. For exceptionally fearful puppies, this process may have to be repeated many times, with the handler always drawing the puppy's attention back and praising and rewarding at the first signs of reduced fear. Always keep in mind that comforting a puppy with petting and soft words during a fear reaction is rewarding and therefore strengthens that undesirable behavior.

THE SICK PUPPY

Note: Sick neonates tend to become hypothermic (below normal body temperature) and must be kept warm in the manner described in the section on physical environment. Food should be withheld until body temperature is normal: 94–97 degrees Fahrenheit up to two weeks; 97–99 degrees Fahrenheit between two and four weeks; after four weeks normal adult temperature of 101–102 degrees Fahrenheit. The digestive system stops functioning below these body temperatures.

A puppy getting the nutrition and calories he needs will sleep most of the time and have a rounded, plump look. An overfed puppy will usually develop diarrhea. If that happens, the next feeding should be halved and then the amount gradually increased by a few drops each feeding, until the recommended amount is reached. If this does not stop the diarrhea, treat as recommended by your veterinarian or as given below. If your pup's stools are too dry and

Any signs of illness in the neonate should be brought to your veterinarian's attention immediately.

Your local pet shop sells excellent grooming supplies, which can sometimes be purchased in affordable combination packages. Photo courtesy of Wahl, USA.

of the puppy and the underlying cause of the dehydration. An *emergency only oral* rehydrating formula for puppies and other mammals, developed by the World Health Organization and passed on to me by Dr. Jefferies, V.M.D. of the Maywood Dog and Cat Hospital, Maywood, California is:

WORLD HEALTH ORGANIZATION ORAL REHYDRATING FORMULA

Mix the following in one quart of water and keep refrigerated until use.

3/4 teaspoon table salt

3/4 teaspoon baking soda

1/3 teaspoon Lite Salt (look in diet/health food section)

3 1/3 tablespoons dextrose (sugar)

Warmed to body temperature, this formula can be given with a syringe or eyedropper, one to three milliliters at a time, every half-hour until the puppy is rehydrated. There are ready-made oral rehydrating products available in flavored or unflavored (use this if possible) versions in the infant sections of most drug stores and food markets.

hard, increase the amount per feeding slightly, or add a few drops of clear Karo syrup to the formula.

A dehydrated puppy will have a "shrunken" look, as if he has too much skin. If, when you pinch up the skin over the back of the neck between a thumb and forefinger, the skin springs right back smoothly, the puppy is getting enough fluids. If the skin remains in a raised "tent," the puppy is dehydrated and must receive easily absorbed fluids. Another sign of dehydration is urine that is thick like honey or orange in color. A veterinarian can prescribe any one of several types of rehydrating fluids, depending on the condition

SYMPTOMS OF PROBLEMS

The signs of illness in a neonate are as follows:

Restlessness and Excessive Crying

A quiet, sleeping puppy that wakes and fusses only when he can be expected to be hungry is acting in a normal manner. Constant crawling around can indicate the puppy is either too hot or cold. If he is too hot, he will breathe through his open mouth. Constant whimpering or repetitive high-pitched cries that go on when the pup has been fed recently and the environment is within acceptable limits indicates a serious problem. Perhaps the puppy is not receiving enough food, or perhaps he has an intestinal upset. Be sure to check for diarrhea. If these causes can be ruled out, then the puppy may have a bacterial or viral infection, which requires immediate veterinary attention.

Limpness

Healthy puppies are firm and have good muscle tone. Sick puppies have a slack feel and have to struggle to move even slowly.

Pale Gums

Puppy gums should be pale to reddish pink. If the gums are almost white, this could indicate that the puppy is under-nourished. Malnourishment can be caused by insufficient food intake (calories), feeding a vitamin or mineral deficient diet, disease, or internal or external parasite infestation.

Bloating

A puppy's abdomen should be slightly rounded when the pup has just fed and then slowly go down as the meal is digested. Some causes of bloating are constipation, mechanical intestinal blockage due to a foreign object, improper elimination due to a congenital deformity of the digestive tract, a bacterial infection, or roundworm infestation. Be sure if the dam is caring for the puppy that she is stimulating him to eliminate properly.

COMMON MEDICAL PROBLEMS OF PUPPIES

Veterinary consultation for the

A well-groomed dog is a happier dog, so don't let cumbersome grooming tools stop you from getting the job done. There are compact, lightweight tools available. Photo courtesy of Wahl, USA.

following disorders *must* be obtained *as soon as possible.*

Abdominal Bloating

If there is a *blue* tinge to the skin of the abdomen there could be an umbilical infection that requires *immediate* antibiotic therapy. A heavy roundworm infection (ascariasis) can also cause a distended abdomen. A puppy's stool should be checked and the puppy wormed according to veterinarian recommendation.

Anal Atresia

Affected puppies have no external anal opening and cannot defecate. Euthanasia is the only humane choice.

Bleeding

A rare disorder that can be seen in newborns in which they may have bloody urine, navel bleeding, and nosebleeds. Veterinarian treatment with vitamin K or plasma clotting factors is required.

Cleft Palate

Affected puppies have an open area in the center of the roof of their mouth. They will regurgitate solid food, and sometimes this defect prevents normal nursing. Reconstructive surgery is the only treatment, so affected puppies are usually euthanized.

Diarrhea

Normal newborn stools are soft, barely formed, yellowish to brown,

A thorough examination of your puppy's eyes, ears, and mouth should be part of his annual checkup.

and can contain curdles of milk. Greenish stools indicate that the food is passing too rapidly through the puppy's digestive system or that there is an infection. White stools indicate total lack of digestion, so contact a veterinarian immediately. Bright yellow indicates an overly acidic stool and in this case, puppies can be given one to three milliliters of milk of magnesia, according to weight, twice daily for one or two days. For true diarrhea, caused by a temporary reaction to overfeeding, one to three milliliters of an over-the-counter milk of bismuth or anti-diarrhea medicine may be administered two to three times daily for two days. If the condition persists for 24 hours, consult a veterinarian because puppies dehydrate quickly. Any puppy with diarrhea should have a stool sample checked for parasites.

Excessive Crying

Often the first sign of illness in a neonate is long bouts of crying and whimpering, sometimes up to 20 minutes or more. If their nutritional and environmental needs are being met, normal puppies sleep peacefully, with occasional twitching and other muscle movements, for about 90 percent of the time, up to around four weeks of age. Excessive vocalization can be a symptom of bacterial or viral infection or of undernourishment.

Open Fontanel

This is a condition in which an area of the skull fails to calcify. Common in domed-skull breeds such as Chihuahuas, this defect sometimes indicates hydrocephalus, a condition where excess fluid builds up pressure in the head, causing multiple severe problems. Some treatment of hydrocephalus is possible in some cases, but life expectancy is short.

Pectorus Excavatum

Some puppies have abnormally flat chests. These puppies may become "swimmers," unable to walk normally due to the angle their front limbs must take. Be sure to have non-slip bedding in the puppy box. This condition is most common in certain short-faced breeds. If the puppy is not up on shaky legs by three weeks

Timely vaccinations are extremely important to your puppy's health. Put your puppy on an immunization schedule as soon as possible.

For the sake of your puppy as well as the health of your family, you should bring your puppy to the veterinarian for regular check-ups.

of age, consult the veterinarian or an experienced breeder for remedial therapy techniques such as hobbling.

Skin Lesions

Crusty hairless spots or small puffy blisters, often on the head or neck, may indicate a staphylococcal infection and are treated with antibacterial cleansing solutions and oral antibiotics.

Spine and Tail Deformities

Kinks in the tail are common in some breeds and in general cause no impairments. The spine should be straight when viewed from above. Curvatures, called *lordosis* or *kyphosis*, should be evaluated by a veterinarian to determine possible functional impairment.

Swollen Eyelids

This is when a puppy's eyes are swollen or still closed when they should be open. This is an indication of infection or conjunctivitis, which could cause permanent damage to the puppy's eyes if not treated.

Swollen Joints

Swollen joints may indicate infection and, if left untreated, could result in degeneration of the joints.

INDEX